Arabic Grammar for Beginners

A simplified and concise book on the subject
of Nahw (Arabic Syntax)

By
Shaykh Mufti Saiful Islām

JKN Publications

First Edition in January 2012 — 3000 copies
Second Edition January 2015 — 3000 copies

ISBN: 978-0-9565504-7-7

British Library Cataloguing in Publication Data
A catalogue record for this book is available from the British Library.

Publisher's Note:

Every care and attention has been put into the production of this book. If however, you find any errors they are our own, for which we seek Allāh's ﷻ for-
giveness and reader's pardon.

Published by:

JKN Publications
118 Manningham Lane
Bradford
West Yorkshire
BD8 7JF
United Kingdom

t: +44 (0) 1274 308 456 l w: www.jkn.org.uk l e: info@jkn.org.uk

Author: Shaykh Mufti Saiful Islām

Printed by Mega Printing in Turkey

"In the Name of Allāh, the Most Beneficent,
the Most Merciful"

Contents

Preface

In the Name of Allāh, the Most Compassionate, the Most Merciful

Many people have the zeal and enthusiasm to learn, speak, read and write Arabic. Most notably it is the language of the Holy Qur'ān and the language of the Holy Prophet ﷺ. Nevertheless, the Arabic language has a set of grammatical rules that must be applied when speaking the language and most of all when attempting to understand and translate the Holy Qur'ān and Ahādeeth.

Arabic Grammar can be divided into two categories: Sarf (Arabic Morphology) generally deals with the conjunction of verbs, prefixing and suffixing letters etc. and Nahw (Arabic Syntax) which mainly deals with the diacritical marks (I'rābs) related to endings.

This compilation is a study of Arabic Grammar on the subject of Nahw in a simplified English format. Many books on this subject have been written in various languages such as Arabic, Persian and Urdu. However, in this day and age there is now a growing demand for this subject to be available in English. Nahw plays a significant role in the Arabic Language as a poet once said:

اَلنَّحْوُ فِي الْكَلَامِ كَالْمِلْحِ فِي الطَّعَامِ

"Nahw in speech is like salt in food"

Hence it is essential for a student who is intrigued to learn the Arabic language to be acquainted with Nahw to avoid making errors.

May Allāh ﷻ reward Shaykh Mufti Saiful Islām immensely for un-
dertaking this task of facilitating a wider readership by presenting
the work in the English language and may Allāh ﷻ prolong his life
so that we can continue to attain benefit from his knowledge and
works.

Mufti Abdul Waheed,
Teacher at Jāmiah Khātamun Nabiyyeen
January 2012/Rabiul-Awwal 1433

Nahw (Syntax)

Definition: A branch of knowledge which directs one towards placing the correct diacritical points (اِعۡرَاب) and letters on the end of words and shows how to join the words to form a complete sentence.

Subject Matter: In this study, the word (اَلۡكَلِمَة) and the sentence (اَلۡكَلَام) will be discussed.

Purpose: The purpose of this knowledge is to acquire the necessary skills of Arabic Grammar and to ultimately understand the Holy Qur'ān and Ahādeeth.

Lesson 1: اَلۡكَلِمَة (The Word)

1) اَللَّفۡظُ (expression) comprises of letters, irrespective of whether it has a meaning or not. If it contains a meaning then it is termed اَلۡمَوۡضُوع "meaningful expression" and if it does not contain any meaning then it is termed اَلۡمُهۡمَل, for instance قَلَمۡ وَلَمۡ; in this example the word قَلَمۡ is اَلۡمَوۡضُوع and the word وَلَمۡ is اَلۡمُهۡمَل.

Since the Arabic language and Grammar is mainly concerned with meaningful words and utterances, our subject matter will only focus on اَلۡمَوۡضُوع.

2) اَللَّفْظُ الْمَوْضُوْع(**Meaningful Expression**) :

There are two types of اَلْمَوْضُوْع:

a) اَلْمُفْرَد or اَلْكَلِمَة i.e. a word. For instance, قَلَمٌ ,كِتَابٌ

b) اَلْمُرَكَّب or اَلْكَلاَم i.e. a group of words e.g. قَرَءَ حَامِدٌ(Hamid read)

3) اَلْكَلِمَة (**The word**) :

There are three types of اَلْكَلِمَة:

a) إِسْمٌ (Noun)

b) فِعْلٌ(Verb)

c) حَرْفٌ (Particle/Letter)

a) إِسْم (**Noun**) - إِسْم is that اَلْكَلِمَة which is independent of other words in conveying its meaning. However, it is devoid of any of the three tenses (past, present and future). For example; قَلَمٌ (pen), كِتَابٌ (book), وَلَدٌ (child).

b) فِعْل (**Verb**) - فِعْل is that اَلْكَلِمَة which is independent of other words in conveying its meaning and it also conveys one of the three tenses i.e. past, present or future. For example; نَصَرَ (He helped), يَنْصُرُ(He is helping/will help), قَرَءَ (He read), يَقْرَءُ (He is reading/will read), كَتَبَ(He wrote), يَكْتُبُ (He is writing/will write).

c) حَرْف (**Particle**) - حَرْف is that اَلْكَلِمَة which is dependent on either an فِعْل ,إِسْم or sometimes both in conveying its meaning. It does not

9

convey any of the three tenses. For example; فِى (in), ثُمَّ (then), مِنُ (from). The following are some examples of the collective usage of all three;

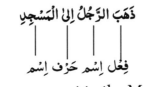

(The man went to the Masjid)

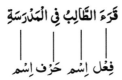

(The student read in the Madrasah)

Exercise

1) Identify the فِعُل, اِسْم and حَرُف in the following sentences:

a) كَتَبَ زَيْدٌ كِتَابًا فِى الْبَيْتِ (Zaid wrote a letter in the house)

b) نَصَرَ حَامِدٌ بَكْرًا فِى الشَّارِعِ (Hamid helped Bakr in the street)

c) رَأَيْتُ كَوْكَبًا فِى السَّمَآءِ (I saw a star in the sky)

2) Give ten examples of اِسْم in a sentence.

3) Give ten examples of فِعُل in a sentence.

4) Give ten examples of حَرُف in a sentence.

Lesson 2: اَلْمُرَكَّب (Compound)

اَلْمُرَكَّب is a combination of two or more words e.g. ذَهَبَ زَيْدٌ (Zaid went). There are two types of اَلْمُرَكَّب;

a) اَلْمُرَكَّبُ التَّام (complete sentence)

b) اَلْمُرَكَّبُ النَّاقِص (incomplete sentence)

a) اَلْمُرَكَّبُ التَّام is a combination of words from which a complete meaning is understood without further explanation. For exam-ple; اَلرَّجُلُ قَائِمٌ (The man is standing), اِشْرَبِ الْمَآءَ (Drink the water), هَلْ فَهِمْتَ الدَّرْسَ (Did you understand the lesson?).

b) اَلْمُرَكَّبُ النَّاقِص is a combination of words that delivers an incomplete meaning. For example; كِتَابُ طَالِبٍ (A student's book), اَلدَّرْسُ السَّهْلُ (Easy lesson), قَلَمِيْ (My pen).

Note: A complete sentence is also called اَلْجُمْلَة or اَلْكَلَامُ.

اَلْكَلَامُ (Sentence)

There are two types of اَلْكَلَامُ:

1) اَلْجُمْلَةُ الْخَبَرِيَّة

2) اَلْجُمْلَةُ الْاِنْشَائِيَّة

1) اَلْجُمْلَةُ الْخَبَرِيَّة is that sentence wherein the possibility of truth or falsehood can exist. For example; اَلتِّلْمِيْذُ مَرِيْضٌ (The student is ill).

2) اَلْجُمْلَةُ الْإِنْشَائِيَّة is that sentence wherein the possibility of truth or falsehood does not exist. For example; اِقْرَأِ الْكِتَابَ (Read the book).

Exercise

1) Mention ten examples of اَلْمُرَكَّبُ التَّام.

2) Mention ten examples of اَلْمُرَكَّبُ النَّاقِص.

3) Identify اَلْمُرَكَّبُ النَّاقِص and اَلْمُرَكَّبُ التَّام in the following sentences.

a) اَلرَّجُلُ الصَّالِحُ   b) ظُلْمَةُ اللَّيْلِ   c) يَوْمُ الدِّيْنِ   d) جَاءَ رَجُلٌ   e) قَعَدَ الطَّالِبُ

f) ذٰلِكَ الْكِتَابُ   g) اِبْنُ الرَّجُلِ عَاقِلٌ   h) ضَرَبَ لَكُمْ مَثَلاً   i) اَلطَّالِبُ الذَّكِيُّ

j) قَتَلَ دَاوُدُ جَالُوْتَ

Lesson 3: اَلْجُمْلَةُ الْخَبَرِيَّة

There are two types of اَلْجُمْلَةُ الْخَبَرِيَّة;

1) اَلْجُمْلَةُ الاِسْمِيَّة

2) اَلْجُمْلَةُ الْفِعْلِيَّة

1) اَلْجُمْلَةُ الاِسْمِيَّة is a sentence which begins with a noun (اِسْم). The first part (subject) of the sentence is called اَلْمُسْنَدُ اِلَيْهِ or اَلْمُبْتَدَا and the second part is called اَلْمُسْنَد or اَلْخَبَر. In both cases the اِعْرَاب will be مَرْفُوْع. For example; زَيْدٌ حَاضِرٌ (Zaid is present), مَحْمُوْدٌ عَالِمٌ (Mahmood is an Ālim). In these two examples زَيْدٌ and مَحْمُوْدٌ are اَلْمُسْنَدُ اِلَيْهِ and اَلْمُبْتَدَا whilst حَاضِرٌ and عَالِمٌ are both اَلْمُسْنَد and اَلْخَبَر.

2) اَلْجُمْلَةُ الْفِعْلِيَّة is a sentence which begins with a فِعْل (verb). The first part of the sentence will be known as اَلْمُسْنَد or فِعْل and the second part will be اَلْمُسْنَدُ اِلَيْهِ or فَاعِل (subject). The فَاعِل will always remain مَرْفُوْع. For example; قَرَأَ حَامِدٌ (Hamid read). In this example قَرَأَ is اَلْمُسْنَد and فِعْل whereas حَامِدٌ is اَلْمُسْنَدُ اِلَيْهِ and فَاعِل. Some other examples are; خَدَعَ الشَّيْطَانُ, (Shaytān deceived), جَعَلَ اللهُ (Allāh made), خَلَقَ اللهُ (Allāh created).

Note: The subject noun, concerning which something is mentioned or of which information is given, is called اَلْمُبْتَدَا or اَلْمُسْنَدُ اِلَيْهِ and the word(s) that gives the information is called اَلْمُسْنَد or اَلْخَبَر.

Exercise

1) Write down ten examples of ٱلْجُمْلَةُ الِاسْمِيَّة.

2) Mention ten examples of ٱلْجُمْلَةُ الْفِعْلِيَّة.

3) Identify ٱلْمُسْنَدُ اِلَيْهِ and ٱلْمُسْنَدُ in the following sentences.

   a) زَيْدٌ حَسَنٌ

   b) نَصَرَ سَعِيدٌ

   c) قَامَ الطَّالِبُ

   d) ٱلْمُدَرِّسُ جَدِيدٌ

   e) اَلْوَلَدُ صَالِحٌ

   f) قَرَءَ الرَّجُلُ

   g) نَفَعَ الاُسْتَاذُ

   h) ٱلْمُهَنْدِسُ ذَكِيٌّ

   i) اَلْقَمَرُ بَعِيدٌ

   j) ضَحِكَ الشَّيْطَانُ

Lesson 4: اَلْجُمْلَةُ الْاِنْشَائِيَّة

There are ten types of اَلْجُمْلَةُ الْاِنْشَائِيَّة;

1) اَلْاَمْرُ (To command) for example; اِضْرِبْ (hit), اَقِمِ الصَّلٰوةَ (Establish Salāh).

2) اَلنَّهْىُ (To prohibit) for example: لاَ تَضْرِبْ (Do not hit), لاَتَرْفَعُوْا اَصْوَاتَكُمْ (Do not raise your voices).

3) اَلْاِسْتِفْهَام (To question) for example; كَيْفَ حَالُكَ (How are you?), اَلَسْتُ بِرَبِّكُمْ (Am I not your Lord?).

4) اَلتَّمَنِّى (To wish) for example; لَيْتَ الشَّبَابَ يَعُوْدُ (If only the youth age returned), لَيْتَنِىْ كُنْتُ تُرَاباً (If only I became dust).

5) اَلتَّرَجِّى (To hope) for example; لَعَلَّ الْمَرِيْضَ نَائِمٌ (Hopefully the sick person is sleeping), لَعَلَّكُمْ تَتَّقُوْنَ (Hopefully you become God-fearing).

Note: The difference between اَلتَّمَنِّى and اَلتَّرَجِّى is that اَلتَّمَنِّى can be used for both possible and impossible things whereas اَلتَّرَجِّى is generally used for something that is attainable.

6) اَلنِّدا (To call) for example; يَاَاللّٰه (O Allāh).

Note: This is a complete sentence.

7) اَلْعَرْضُ (To request) for example; اَلَاتَجْتَهِدُ فَتَفُوْزَ (Aren't you going to try hard so that you become successful), اَلَايَعْلَمُ مَنْ خَلَقَ (Doesn't he know who created him).

Note: The difference between اَلْاِسْتِفْهَام and اَلْعَرْضُ is that in the former (اَلْاِسْتِفْهَام) an answer is required, whereas the latter (اَلْعَرْضُ)

15

is a mere request or proposal but no answer is anticipated.

8) اَلْقَسْمُ (An oath) for example: وَالله (By Allāh), تَاللهِ إِنَّكَ لَفِيْ ضَلَلِكَ الْقَدِيْمِ (By Allāh! Indeed you are in your old mistake).

9) اَلتَّعَجُّب (Amazement) for example; مَا أَحْسَنَ زَيْدًا (How good is Zaid), قُتِلَ الْإِنْسَانُ مَا أَكْفَرَه (Let man be destroyed, how ungrateful he is).

10) اَلْعُقُوْدُ (Transaction/Pledge) for example; The seller says in the transaction; بِعْتُ هَذَا الْكِتَابَ (I have sold this book to you) and in return the buyer says; اِشْتَرَيْتُهُ (I have purchased it).

Note: In the above examples of اَلْعُقُوْدُ it may seem to be a اَلْخَبَرِيَّة, however in Islamic law, a contract is binding on both parties, so there can be no question of truth and falsehood. Therefore, such a statement will be classed as اِنْشَائِيَّة. Nevertheless, if someone informs you of having bought the book and says (I have purchased this book) then this statement will become اَلْخَبَرِيَّة.

Exercise

1) Give three examples of each type of اَلْجُمْلَةُ الْإِنْشَائِيَّة.

2) Identify which type of اَلْجُمْلَةُ الْإِنْشَائِيَّة the following sentences are;

3) يَا عَبْدَ اللهِ

4) لَعَلَّ زَيْدًا حَاضِرٌ

5) مَتَى تَذْهَبُ

a) اِضْرِبْ بِعَصَاكَ الْحَجَرَ

b) لَا تَجْعَلْ يَدَكَ مَغْلُوْلَةً إِلَى عُنُقِكَ

1) لَيْتَنِىْ لَمْ اَتَّخِذْ فُلَانًا خَلِيْلًا

2) اَسْمِعْ بِهِمْ وَاَبْصِرْ

3) تَاﷲِ لَاَكِيْدَنَّ اَصْنَامَكُمْ

4) اَلَا تَأْتِيْنِىْ فَاُعْطِيَكَ دِيْنَارًا

5) يَاحَيُّ يَاقَيُّوْمُ

Lesson 5: اَلْمُرَكَّبُ النَّاقِص
(Incomplete sentence)

There are several types of incomplete sentences:

1) اَلْمُرَكَّبُ التَّوْصِيْفِى - (The descriptive phrase)

2) اَلْمُرَكَّبُ الْاِضَافِى - (The phrase that shows possession)

3) اَلْمُرَكَّبُ الْاِشَارِى - (The demonstrative phrase)

4) اَلْمُرَكَّبُ الْبِنَائِى - (The numerical phrase)

5) مُرَكَّبُ مَنْعِ الصَّرْف - (The indeclinable phrase)

1) اَلْمُرَكَّبُ التَّوْصِيْفِى - is that اَلْمُرَكَّبُ (compound) in which the second word describes the first word. The first word is called اَلْمَنْعُوْت and the second word is called اَلنَّعْت. For example; رَجُلٌ صَالِحٌ (A pious man), in this example the word صَالِحٌ is the describing word which is called اَلنَّعْت and the first word رَجُلٌ is the subject that is being described which is called اَلْمَنْعُوْت.

2) اَلْمُرَكَّبُ الْاِضَافِى - is that اَلْمُرَكَّبُ which generally shows possession i.e. the second word possesses the first word. The first word will be

17

called اَلْمُضَاف and the second word اَلْمُضَافُ إِلَيْه. For example; كِتَابُ زَيْدٍ (Zaid's book). In this example the word كِتَابُ is the اَلْمُضَاف and زَيْد the اَلْمُضَافُ إِلَيْه.

3) اَلْمُرَكَّبُ الْإِشَارِى - is that اَلْمُرَكَّبُ wherein the first word, the pronoun, is used to indicate towards the second word. The pronoun is known as اِسْمُ الْإِشَارَة and the second word اَلْمُشَارُ إِلَيْه. For example, هٰذَا الْكِتَابُ (This book). In this example the word هٰذَا is اِسْمُ الْإِشَارَة and الْكِتَابُ is اَلْمُشَارُ إِلَيْه.

Note: اَلْمُشَارُ إِلَيْه must be prefixed with اَل for the sentence to be incomplete. If it is not prefixed with اَل then the sentence structure will be called اَلْمُرَكَّبُ التَّامِ (complete sentence). For example; هٰذَا كِتَابٌ (This is a book). In this case هٰذَا will become the اَلْمُبْتَدَا and كِتَابٌ will become اَلْخَبَر.

4) اَلْمُرَكَّبُ الْبِنَائِى - is that اَلْمُرَكَّبُ wherein two words are combined together to form a single word. A conjunction (حَرْف عَطْف) originally linked the two words. For example; أَحَدَ عَشَرَ which was originally أَحَدٌ وَعَشَرٌ. This is only found in the numbers between 11 -19.

5) اَلْمُرَكَّبُ مَنْعِ الصَّرْف - is that اَلْمُرَكَّبُ wherein two words are combined to form one word. اَلْحَرْفُ الْعَطْف (conjunction) did not originally exist between the two words. For example; بَعْلَبَكُّ (a name of a city). This was formed by combining the word بَعْل (name of an idol) and بَكّ (name of a king).

18

Exercise

1) Give ten examples of اَلْمُرَكَّبُ التَّوْصِيفِي and اَلْمُرَكَّبُ الْاِضَافِي.

2) Give five examples of اَلْمُرَكَّبُ الْاِشَارِى, اَلْمُرَكَّبُ الْبِنَائِى and مُرَكَّبُ مَنْعِ الصَّرْفِ.

Lesson 6:
عَلَامَاتُ الْاِسْمِ (Signs of a Noun)

The اِسْم (noun) can be identified by observing any of the following signs:

1) An 'ال' is prefixed at the beginning of the word e.g. اَلْقَلَمُ.

2) It is preceded with اَلْحَرْفُ الْجَرّ e.g. مِنَ الْمَدْرَسَةِ.

3) The last letter may have a Tanween e.g. كِتَابٌ.

4) It can be اَلْمُسْنَدُ اِلَيْهِ (subject) e.g. زَيْدٌ حَاضِرٌ.

5) It can be اَلْمُضَاف e.g. كِتَابُ زَيْدٍ.

6) It can be اَلتَّثْنِيَه (dual) e.g. رَجُلَانِ.

7) It can be اَلْجَمْع (plural) e.g. رِجَالٌ.

Note: In the case of a dual and a plural scale of فِعْل (verb), it must be noted that the action is one whilst the doers are two or more. Hence dual and plural are features of an اِسْم and not of a فِعْل.

1) It can be اَلْمَنْعُوت e.g. رَجُلٌ صَالِحٌ.

2) It can be suffixed with a round ة e.g. مَدِيْنَةٌ.

3) It can be اَلْمُنَادَى e.g. يَا رَجُلُ.

19

4) It can be اَلْمُصَغَّر (diminutive form) e.g. رُجَيْلٌ (a small man).

5) It can be اَلْاِسْمُ الْمَنْسُوْب (related noun) e.g. بَغْدَادِيّ (a Baghdadian).

عَلَامَاتُ الْفِعْلِ (The Signs of a Verb)

The فِعْل can be identified by observing any of the following signs:

1) It can be preceded with قَدْ, e.g. قَدْ كَتَبَ (He has surely written).

2) The word is preceded with the letter س or سَوْفَ e.g. سَيَكْتُبُ (He will soon write), سَوْفَ يَكْتُبُ (He will write afterwards).

3) It can be preceded with a اَلْحَرْفُ الْجَازِم e.g. لَمْ يَكْتُبْ.

4) It can be اَلْاَمْر (order) e.g. اُكْتُبْ (You write).

5) It can come as اَلنَّهْى (prohibition) e.g. لاَ تَكْتُبْ (Don't write).

6) It can contain اَلضَّمِيْر (hidden pronoun) e.g. كَتَبَ (He wrote).

7) It can be preceded with اَلْحَرْفُ النَّاصِب e.g. لَنْ يَكْتُبَ (He will never write).

8) It can contain تَا التَّانِيْث at the end e.g. كَتَبَتْ (She wrote).

عَلَامَاتُ الْحَرْف (The Signs of a Particle)

The basic signs for a حَرْف is that which doesn't accept the features of اِسْم and فِعْل. It is rather used to join two words together. There are three categories:

1) Joining two nouns together e.g. زَيْدٌ فِي الدَّارِ (Zaid is in the house).
2) Joining two verbs together e.g. أُرِيْدُ اَنْ اَتْلُوَا الْقُرْاٰنَ (I intend to recite the Qur'ān).
3) Joining a verb and a noun together e.g. كَتَبْتُ بِالْقَلَمِ (I wrote with a pen).

Lesson 7: Types of Nouns

Nouns are of two types:

1) اَلْمَعْرِفَة - Definite Noun
2) اَلنَّكِرَة - Indefinite Noun

1) اَلْمَعْرِفَة (Definite Noun) refers to a specific thing, for instance مَكَّة, عُمَرُ etc which are specific names or اَلرَّجُلُ which refers to a specific man.

2) اَلنَّكِرَة (Indefinite Noun) is a word that refers to something in general without any specification. For instance, رَجُلٌ (a man), it refers to any man or the word طَيِّبٌ which refers to any good thing in general.

21

The types of اَلْمَعْرِفَة (Definite Nouns)

اَلْمَعْرِفَةis of seven types:

1) اَلضَّمَائِر(Personal Pronouns) - These are pronouns which refer to the first, second and third person. Some examples are; اَنَا(I), اَنْتَ (you), هُوَ(he), هِيَ(she).

2) اَلْعَلَم(Proper Noun) - That noun which refers to the name of a specific person, place or thing. For instance; زَيْدٌ, مَكَّةٌ, زَمْزَمُ.

3) اِسْمُ الْإِشَارَة (Demonstrative Noun) - That noun which is used to demonstrate or point out to something or someone. For example; هٰذا (this), ذٰلك(that).

4) اَلْاِسْمُ الْمَوْصُوْل (Relative Pronoun) - That noun which is used to relate or connect the sentence that follows it. Some examples of words used are; اَلَّذِئ (masculine; that which), اَلَّتِئ (feminine; that which), اَلَّذِيْنَ(those which).

5) اَلْمُنَادٰى (Vocative) - That noun which follows اَلْحَرُفُ النِّدا. For example; يَارَجُلُ(O Man).

6) اَلْمُعَرَّف بِأَلْThat noun which has been prefixed with اَل (definitive particle). For example; اَلْكِتَاب (The book).

7) اَلْمُضَاف إِلَى الْمَعْرِفَة- That common noun which is related to any of the above mentioned definite nouns (except اَلْمُنَادٰى) in such a way that the second noun (اَلْمَعْرِفَة) possesses the first (اَلنَّكِرَة). For example: كِتَابُكَ (your book), كِتَابُ زَيْدٍ (Zaid's book), كِتَابُ الَّذِى (the

book of the person who), كِتَابُ هٰذَا الرَّجُلِ(this man's book), كِتَابُ الطَّالِبِ (the student's book).

Exercise

1) Give five examples of each definite noun.

2) Identify which of the following is أَلْمَعْرِفَة and which is أَلنَّكِرَة. Also mention which type it is.

a) كِتَابٌ b) أَلرَّسُوْلُ c) زَيْدٌ d) قَلَمٌ e) قَلَمُكَ f) أَلَّتِيْ g) أَلْإِنْسَانُ h) يَارَجُلُ i) أَنْتَ j) كِتَابُ هٰذَا الرَّجُلِ k) حَافِظٌ

Lesson 8: The Particles of أَلتَّعْرِيْف and أَلتَّنْكِيْر.

The particles of أَلتَّعْرِيْف and أَلتَّنْكِيْر are as follows;

1) Tanween is generally attached to the end of a word that is أَلتَّنْكِيْر (Indefinite). It is usually translated as 'a' or 'an'. For example; رَجُلٌ(a man), تُفَّاحٌ(an apple), مَاءٌ(water).

   Note: Sometimes a proper noun also has a Tanween e.g. زَيْدٌ, مُحَمَّدٌ.

2) The letters ال (Alif-Lām) are called حَرْفُ التَّعْرِيْف or لَامُ التَّعْرِيْف in Arabic. It is generally translated as 'the' in English. For example; أَلْكِتَابُ(the book).

3) When ال is prefixed to a word that has a Tanween on it then the Tanween will drop i.e. rather than two Dhammas it will become one Dhamma. For example; رَجُلٌwill become أَلرَّجُلُ.

23

4) When ال appears before an اِسْم that commences with اَلْحُرُوفُ الشَّمْسِيَّة (the letters of Shamsiyya) then the لام of ال will not be pronounced. For example; اَلرَّجُلُ is pronounced as Ar-Rajulu and not Al-Rajulu. The opposite will apply to اَلْحُرُوفُ القَمَرِيَّة(the letters of Qamariyya) for example; اَلْكِتَابُ is pronounced as Al-Kitābu rather than Ak-Kitābu. The letters of Shams are: ت ث د ذ ر ز س ش ص ض ط ظ ل ن

The letters of Qamar are; ا ب ج ح خ ع غ ف ق ك م و ه ى

5) If any word precedes that word which has ال then the first word is joined to the لام of the second word and pronounced by joining it. The Hamzah in the ال will be called Hamzatul-Wasl. The Hamzah will not be pronounced. For example; بَابُ البَيْتِ(the door of the house). It is incorrect to read بَابُ اَلْبَيْتِ i.e. pronouncing the Alif in the ال.

6) If one word ends with a Sukoon and the other begins with a Sukoon also, then this is called اِجْتِمَاعُ السَّاكِنَيْن(two Sukoons meeting together). In this case the first Sukoon will change into a Kasra. For example; أُنْصُرْ الوَلَدَ will be pronounced as أُنْصُرِ الوَلَدَ. The Hamzatul Wasl (connecting Hamzah) before the ل will not be pronounced although it is still written.

Exercise

1) After prefixing ال, state which of the following words are اَلشَّمْسِيَّة and which are اَلقَمَرِيَّة.

    a) كِتَابٌ b) إِنْسَانٌ c) بَيْتٌ d) دِيْكٌ e) ذَهَبٌ f) جَنَّةٌ g) وَلَدٌ h) شَمْسٌ (i
    زَهَرَةٌ (j تِلْمِيْذٌ k) خُبْزٌ l) ثَوْبٌ

2) Give five examples of ال where Hamzatul Wasl is not pronounced.

3) Give five examples of اِجْتِمَاعُ السَّاكِنَيْنِ and how it should be written.

Lesson 9: Masculine and Feminine Gender.

1) Arabic words are of two types with regards to gender:

   a) اَلْمُذَكَّر - Masculine i.e. اِبْنٌ

   b) اَلْمُؤَنَّث - Feminine i.e. اِبْنَةٌ

اَلْمُذَكَّر - (Masculine gender) is that word which has no signs of اَلتَّأنِيْث (feminine).

اَلْمُؤَنَّث - Feminine gender can be identified in any of the following two ways:

1) اَلْمُؤَنَّث بِالْقِيَاس- (Deduced by a set of rules)

2) اَلْمُؤَنَّث بِالسِّمَاع- (The common usage of the word)

3) اَلْمُؤَنَّث بِالْقِيَاسis further divided into two categories:

  a) اَلْمُؤَنَّث اللَّفْظِى

  b) اَلْمُؤَنَّث الْمَعْنَوِى

اَلْمُؤَنَّث اللَّفْظِى

اَلْمُؤَنَّث اللَّفْظِىis that feminine noun in which any of the following three signs (علامات التأنيث) are found:

  (i) ة (Tā) appears, even on a masculine proper noun. For example: عَائِشَةُ طَلْحَةُ جَمِيْلَةٌ حَافِظَةٌ عَالِمَةٌ.

a) (ii) اَلْاَلِفُ الْمَقْصُوْرَة - An Alif Maqsoorah appears at the end of a word. Alif Maqsoorah is an Alif which is read without prolonging on the word and which has no Hamzah after it. For example; حُبْلٰی (pregnant woman), بُشْرٰی (name of a girl).

(iii) اَلْاَلِفُ الْمَمْدُوْدَة - An Alif Mamdoodah appears at the end of the word. Alif Mamdoodah is an Alif which is pronounced by prolonging it on that feminine word and has a Hamzah after it. For example; حَمْرَاء (red complexion woman), حَسْنَاء (beautiful woman), زَهْرَاء (radiant).

اَلْمُؤَنَّثُ الْمَعْنَوِی

اَلْمُؤَنَّثُ الْمَعْنَوِی is that feminine noun in which none of the above mentioned signs are found. However, the word itself implies the feminine gender. This can be identified by any of the following;

(i) Name of a female, for example; مَرْیَمُ زَیْنَبُ

(ii) Words that denote feminine gender, for example; اُمٌّ اُخْتٌ

(iii) Names of cities, countries, towns etc, for example; قُرَیْشٌ بَغْدَادُ مِصْرُ بَاكِسْتَان

(iv) Names of body parts that are in pairs, for example; یَدٌ رِجْلٌ عَیْنٌ اُذُنٌ

2) اَلْمُؤَنَّث بِالسِّمَاع is of two types;

a) اَلْمُؤَنَّث بِعَلَامَةٍ مُقَدَّرَة - is that feminine in which the sign is hidden. This is established by looking at اَلْمُصَغَّر (diminutive form) of a particular word, since this is how the original letters of a word are established in the Arabic language. For example; اَرْضٌ(earth) is the normal word and اُرَیْضَةٌ is its اَلْمُصَغَّر, similarly شَمْسٌ (sun) is the normal word and شُمَیْسَةٌ is its اَلْمُصَغَّر.

b) اَلْمُؤَنَّث بِاِسْتِعْمَالِ الْعَرَب - is that feminine which is purely based on the usage of the Arabs in their conversations. There is no specific rule applied in this. For example; نَارٌ (fire), اِبِلٌ(camel), قِدْرٌ (pot), بِئْرٌ(well), دَلْوٌ(bucket), نَفْسٌ(soul), عَقْرَبٌ(scorpion).

Exercise

b) Give five examples of all types of اَلْمُؤَنَّث.

Lesson 10: اَلْمَبْنِى and اَلْمُعْرَب

In the Arabic language, the اِعْرَاب (diacritical marks) situated at the end of the word is of two types;

1) اَلْمُعْرَب - is that word which accepts all اِعْرَاب at the end of it in accordance with the عَامِل (governing word). For example:

    a) ذَهَبَ زَيْدٌ (Zaid went)

    b) رَأَيْتُ زَيْداً (I saw Zaid)

    c) مَرَرْتُ بِزَيْدٍ (I passed by Zaid)

1)**Note:** In all of the above cases the اِعْرَاب of the letter Dāl has changed.

2) اَلْمَبْنِى - is that word which never changes, it remains the same at all times regardless of what the عَامِل is. For example:

    a) جَآءَ هٰؤُلَآءِ (These people came)

    b) رَأَيْتُ هٰؤُلَآءِ (I saw these people)

    c) مَرَرْتُ بِهٰؤُلَآءِ (I passed by these people)

Note: The اِعْرَاب of the Hamzah in هٰؤُلَآءِ has not changed.

29

اَلْمَبْنٰى

The following words are اَلْمَبْنٰى;

All Huroof (letters) are اَلْمَبْنٰى e.g. اِنَّ .

1) اَلْفِعْلُ الْمَاضِى e.g. كَتَبَ.

2) اَلْاَمْرُ الْحَاضِرُ الْمَعْرُوْف e.g. اُكْتُبْ.

3) اَلْفِعْلُ الْمُضَارِع to which the noon of اَلتَّاكِيْد, whether it is اَلْخَفِيْفَة or اَلثَّقِيْلَة, or the noon of the feminine plural, are suffixed. e.g. لَيَكْتُبَنَّ or يَكْتُبْنَ.

4) اِسْم غَيْرِ الْمُتَمَكِّن (indeclinable nouns) e.g. اَنْتَ and اَلَّذِى.

30

Lesson 11: The types of اَلْمَبْنِى

There are eight types of اَلْمَبْنِى :

1) اَلضَّمَائِر (Pronouns) - There are in total seventy pronouns which
   are divided into five categories.

    a) 14- اَلضَّمِيْرُ الْمَرْفُوْعُ الْمُتَّصِل

    b) 14- اَلضَّمِيْرُ الْمَرْفُوْع الْمُنْفَصِل

    c) 14- اَلضَّمِيْرُ الْمَنْصُوْب الْمُتَّصِل

    d) 14- اَلضَّمِيْرُ الْمَنْصُوْب الْمُنْفَصِل

    e) 14- اَلضَّمِيْرُ الْمَجْرُوْر الْمُتَّصِل

اَلضَّمَائِر have two forms; the first is that pronoun which is apparent
and has an exclusive form which is called بَارِز. The second form is
that pronoun which is hidden within the فِعْل. This is known as
مُسْتَتَر.See the table on the following page.

اَلضَّمِيْرُ الْمَجْرُوْر	اَلضَّمِيْرُ الْمَنْصُوْب		اَلضَّمِيْرُ الْمَرْفُوْعُ	
الْمُتَّصِل	الْمُنْفَصِل	الْمُتَّصِل	الْمُنْفَصِل	الْمُتَّصِل
لَهُ	إِيَّاهُ	نَصَرْتُهُ	هُوَ	ضَرَبَ
لَهُمَا	إِيَّاهُمَا	نَصَرْتُهُمَا	هُمَا	ضَرَبَا
لَهُمْ	إِيَّاهُمْ	نَصَرْتُهُمْ	هُمْ	ضَرَبُوْا
لَهَا	إِيَّاهَا	نَصَرْتُهَا	هِيَ	ضَرَبَتْ
لَهُمَا	إِيَّاهُمَا	نَصَرْتُهُمَا	هُمَا	ضَرَبَتَا
لَهُنَّ	إِيَّاهُنَّ	نَصَرْتُهُنَّ	هُنَّ	ضَرَبْنَ
لَكَ	إِيَّاكَ	نَصَرْتُكَ	أَنْتَ	ضَرَبْتَ
لَكُمَا	إِيَّاكُمَا	نَصَرْتُكُمَا	أَنْتُمَا	ضَرَبْتُمَا
لَكُمْ	إِيَّاكُمْ	نَصَرْتُكُمْ	أَنْتُمْ	ضَرَبْتُمْ
لَكِ	إِيَّاكِ	نَصَرْتُكِ	أَنْتِ	ضَرَبْتِ
لَكُمَا	إِيَّاكُمَا	نَصَرْتُكُمَا	أَنْتُمَا	ضَرَبْتُمَا
لَكُنَّ	إِيَّاكُنَّ	نَصَرْتُكُنَّ	أَنْتُنَّ	ضَرَبْتُنَّ
لِيْ	إِيَّايَ	نَصَرْتَنِيْ	أَنَا	ضَرَبْتُ
لَنَا	إِيَّانَا	نَصَرْتَنَا	نَحْنُ	ضَرَبْنَا

32

2) اَسْمَاءُ الْإِشَارَة (Demonstrative Pronouns) - That noun which is used to demonstrate or point towards something or someone.

		Showing Nearness اَسْمَاءُ الْإِشَارَةِ لِلْقَرِيب			Showing Distance اَسْمَاءُ الْإِشَارَةِ لِلْبَعِيد
هٰذَا	Masculine	This (one person)	ذٰلِكَ	Masculine	That (one person)
هٰذَانِ		These (dual) حالة الرفع	ذَانِكَ		Those (dual) حالة الرفع
هٰذَيْنِ		These (dual) حالة النصب والجر	ذَيْنِكَ		Those (dual) حالة النصب والجر
هٰؤُلَاءِ		These (plural)	أُولَائِكَ		Those (plural)
هٰذِهِ	Feminine	This (one person)	تِلْكَ	Feminine	That (one person)
هَاتَانِ		These (dual) حالة الرفع	تَانِكَ		Those (dual) حالة الرفع
هَاتَيْنِ		These (dual) حالة النصب والجر	تَيْنِكَ		Those (dual) حالة النصب والجر
هٰؤُلَاءِ		These (plural)	أُولَائِكَ		Those (plural)

Some examples are as follows:

هٰذَا رَجُلٌ	ذَالِكَ وَلَدٌ
هٰذَانِ رَجُلَانِ	ذَانِكَ وَلَدَانِ
هٰؤُلَاءِ رِجَالٌ	أُولَائِكَ أَوْلَادٌ

هٰذِهِ بِنْتٌ	تِلْكَ اِمْرَأَةٌ
هَاتَانِ بِنْتَانِ	تَانِكَ اِمْرَأَتَانِ
هٰؤُلَاءِ بَنَاتٌ	أُولَائِكَ نِسَاءٌ

3) اَلْأَسْمَاءُ الْمَوْصُولَة (The Relative Pronouns) - Those nouns which have to be connected or related to the sentence following it. اَلْاِسْمُ الْمَوْصُول requires a صِلَه in order to become a complete sentence. The صِلَه is usually the explanation of اَلْاِسْمُ الْمَوْصُول and can be اَلْجُمْلَة الْخَبَرِيَّة that consists of a ضَمِيْر (pronoun) referring back to اَلْاِسْمُ الْمَوْصُول. This is illustrated through the following example;

قَدْ سَمِعَ اللهُ قَوْلَ الَّتِى تُجَادِلُكَ

(Indeed Allāh ﷺ has heard the statement of the woman who was disputing with you). In this example, the word الَّتِى is اَلْاِسْمُ الْمَوْصُول and تُجَادِلُكَ is the صِلَه which is اَلْجُمْلَة الْخَبَرِيَّة. The اَلْجُمْلَة الْخَبَرِيَّة consists of a feminine pronoun (هِى) which is referring back to الَّتِى.

The different types of اَلْأَسْمَاءُ الْمَوْصُولَة are as follows:

34

اَلَّذِى	Masculine	He, who, that, which, that which
اَلَّذَانِ		Those, who, who that, which (dual) حَالةالرفع
اَلَّذَينِ		Those who حَالةالنصبوالجر
اَلَّذِينَ		Those who (plural)

اَلَّتِى	Feminine	She who, who, that, which, that which
اَلَّتَانِ		Those, who, who that, which (dual) حَالةالرفع
اَلَّتَينِ		Those who حَالةالنصبوالجر
اَلَّاتِى		Those who (plural)
اَللَّوَاتِى		Those who (plural)

مَا	That, which, what (generally used with non-humans)
مَنْ	He, she, whose, whom (generally used for humans)
اَلْ	In the meaning of اَلَّذِى and اَلَّتِى
اَىٌّ	In the meaning of اَلَّذِى when attached to اسمالفاعل or اسمالمفعول
اَيَّةٌ	In the meaning of اَلَّتِى
ذُو	In the meaning of اَلَّذِى

35

4) اَسْمَاءُ الْاَفْعَال -These are two types;

a) Those nouns that indicate اَلْمَاضِى (past tense). Such nouns give their اِسْم a Dhamma. These are;

اسماء الافعال	Similar verb	Meaning	Example
هَيْهَاتَ	بَعُدَ	To be far from and remote	هَيْهَاتَ زَيْدٌ Zaid became further away
شَتَّانَ	اِفْتَرَقَ	To separate	شَتَّانَ زَيْدٌ وَ عُمَرُ Zaid and Umar separated
سَرْعَانَ	اَسْرَعَ	To hasten	سَرْعَانَ زَيْدٌ Zaid hastened

b) Those nouns that denote اَلْاَمْرُ الْحَاضِر (command tense). Such nouns give their اِسْم a Fatha. These are;

اسماء الافعال	Similar verb	Meaning	Example
رُوَيْدَ	اَمْهِلْ	To grant respite	رُوَيْدَ زَيْدًا Give respite to Zaid
بَلْهَ	دَعْ	To leave	بَلْهَ زَيْدًا Leave Zaid
حَيَّهَلْ	اِئْتِ	Come, hasten, bring forth	حَيَّهَلِ الطَّعَامَ Bring the food
هَلُمَّ	اِئْتِ	Come, hasten	هَلُمَّ زَيْدًا Come Zaid
دُوْنَكَ	خُذْ	Take	دُوْنَكَ الطَّعَامَ Take the food
عَلَيْكَ	اَلْزِمْ	It is necessary upon you	عَلَيْكَ الرِّفْقَ Hold firm to leniency

5) اَسْمَآءُ الاَصْوَاتِ - Those nouns which are used to express various sounds. Some examples are;

a) كَعْ - Expression used to reprimand a child

b) نَخْ - Expression used to make a camel kneel

c) بَخْ - Expression used to show pleasure or happiness

d) غَاقِ - Expressing the crowing of a crow

e) اُحْ اُحْ - Expressing a cough

f) اُفٌّ - Expressing pain or sorrow

6) اَسْمَآءُ الظُّرُوفِ - Those nouns that are used to show place or time. That noun which is used to show time is called اَلظَّرْفُ الزَّمَانُ. For example; اَيَّانَ (when), اَلآنَ (now).

That noun which indicates to a place is called اَلظَّرْفُ الْمَكَانُ. For example; اَيْنَ (where), عِنْدَ (by, at, near).

7) اَسْمَآءُ الْكِنَايَاتِ - Those nouns that indicate unclear and vague words. These are of two types: the first are كَمْ and كَذَا (so much, so many). These nouns usually denote quantity. The second type are كَيْتَ وَ ذَيْتَ (so and so, such and such) used in daily conversation.

8) اَلْمُرَكَّبُ الْبِنَائِىُ - The numerical nouns, these have been previously discussed in lesson five.

اَلْاَسْمَآءُ الْمُعْرَبَةُ :Lesson 12

اِعْرَابٌ is of two types:

a) اَلْاِعْرَابُ بِالْحَرَكَت- i.e. Dhamma (Pesh), Fatha (Zabar) and Kasra (Zer).

b) اَلْاِعْرَابُ بِالْحَرْف- i.e. Waw in the place of Dhamma, Alif in the place of Dhamma and Fatha, and Yā in the place of Fatha and Kasra.

اِعْرَاب of اِسْم :اِسْم consists of Dhamma, Fatha and Kasra and the اِعْرَاب of فِعْل (verb) has Dhamma, Fatha and Jazm. Generally when an اِسْم has a Dhamma it is called Marfoo, when it has a Fatha it is called Mansoob and when it has a Kasra it is called Maksoor. When a فِعْل has a Dhamma it is called Marfoo, when it has a Fatha it is called Mansoob and when it has a Jazm it is called Majzoom.

In relation to the اِعْرَاب of اَلْاَسْمَآءُ الْمُعْرَبَةُ, there are 16 types. Each one will be discussed below.

1) اَلْمُفْرَدُ الْمُنْصَرِفُ الصَّحِيْح- That independent noun which does not end with a واو or يَاء and is not غَيْرُ الْمُنْصَرِف.

حَالَةُ الرَّفْع	جَاءَنِىْ زَيْدٌ
حَالَةُ النَّصْب	رَأَيْتُ زَيْدًا
حَالَةُ الْجَرّ	مَرَرْتُ بِزَيْدٍ

39

2) اَلْمُفْرَدُ الْقَائِمُ الْمُقَامَ الصَّحِيْح - That independent noun which ends with a واو or ياء preceded with a Sukoon. For example;

حَالَةُ الرَّفْع	هٰذِه دَلْوٌ, هٰذِه ظَبْيٌ
حَالَةُ النَّصْب	رَاَيْتُ دَلْواً, رَاَيْتُ ظَبْياً
حَالَةُ الْجَرّ	مَرَرْتُ بِدَلْوٍ, مَرَرْتُ بِظَبْيٍ

3) اَلْجَمْعُ الْمُكَسَّرُ الْمُنْصَرِفُ - That plural wherein the sequence of the letters of its singular form is 'broken'. Below are some examples;

حَالَةُ الرَّفْع	هٰذِه كُتُبٌ, هٰؤُلَاءِ رِجَالٌ
حَالَةُ النَّصْب	رَاَيْتُ كُتُباً, رَاَيْتُ رِجَالاً
حَالَةُ الْجَرّ	جِئْتُ بِكُتُبٍ, لِلرِّجَالِ نَصِيْبٌ

Note: In these three examples, the noun will get a Dhamma in the state of Raf'a, Fatha in the state of Nasb and Kasra in the state of Jarr.

4) اَلْجَمْعُ الْمُؤَنَّثُ السَّالِم - That feminine plural wherein the sequence of its singular form remains sound and 'unbroken'. For example:

40

حَالَةُ الرَّفْعِ	هُنَّ مُسْلِمَاتٌ
حَالَةُ النَّصْبِ	رَأَيْتُ مُسْلِمَاتٍ
حَالَةُ الْجَرِّ	مَرَرْتُ بِمُسْلِمَاتٍ

Note: In the above examples the noun will get a Dhamma in the state of Raf'a, and Kasra in the state of Nasb and Jarr.

5) غَيْرُ الْمُنْصَرِف - When an اِسْمُ الْمُعْرَب contains any two of the following nine causes or one such cause that is equivalent to two, then such a noun will be said to be غَيْرُ الْمُنْصَرِف. These nine causes are known as اَسْبَابُ مَنْعِ الصَّرْف which are as follows;

a) اَلْعَدْل - This is a noun that has changed its original form to adopt a new one, e.g. عُمَرُ was originally عَامِرٌ.

b) اَلْوَصْف - A noun that is not originally meant for اِسْمُ الذَّات but rather it is a describing word, e.g. اَحْمَرُ (red), اَسْوَدُ (black).

c) اَلتَّأْنِيْث - A noun that has the characteristics of اَلتَّأْنِيْث (feminine) or it is اَلْمُؤَنَّثُ الْمَعْنَوِيُّ, e.g. عَائِشَةُ، فَاطِمَةُ، طَلْحَةُ، مَكَّةُ، زَيْنَبُ، حَمْرَاءُ.

d) اَلْعُجْمَة - A non-Arabic word, e.g. اِبْرَاهِيْمُ.

e) اَلْمَعْرِفَة (اَلْعَلَم) - Name of a person, place or thing, e.g. اِسْمَاعِيْلُ، زَمْزَمُ، مَكَّةُ.

f) اَلْجَمْع - (Plural) This relates exclusively to a particular scale of plural where the first two letters have a Fatha and the third letter is an Alif, e.g. مَسَاجِدُ، مَصَابِيْحُ.

41

g) اَلتَّرْكِيْبُ - A combination of two nouns to form one word, e.g. قَاضِيْخَان ,بَعْلَبَكُّ.

h) اَلْاَلِفُ وَالنُّوْنُ اَلزَّائِدَتَان - That noun to which the letters اَلِف and نُوْن are suffixed, e.g. عُثْمَانُ ,سَلْمَانُ ,رَمَضَانُ.

i) وَزْنُ الْفِعْل - This relates to a noun which is on the scale of a verb, e.g. اَحْمَدُ on the scale of اَفْعَلُ ,اِثْمِدٌ on the scale of اِجْلِسْ.

The اِعْرَاب of غَيْرُ الْمُنْصَرِف in the state of Raf'a, it will be given a Dhamma without a Tanween and in the state of Nasb and Jarr it will be given a Fatha. No Kasra can appear on a غَيْرُ الْمُنْصَرِف word, e.g. مَرَرْتُ بِعُمَرَ ,رَاَيْتُ عُمَرَ ,جَآءَ عُمَرُ.

Note: A غَيْرُ الْمُنْصَرِف word will not have a Tanween but with regards to a Kasra there are some exceptional cases;

a) When it is a مُضَاف , e.g. صَلَّيْتُ فِىْ مَسَاجِدِكُمْ.

b) When the noun is prefixed with ال, e.g. صَلَّيْتُ فِى الْمَسَاجِدِ كُلِّهَا

6) اَلْاَسْمَآءُ السِّتَّةُ الْمُكَبَّرَة - Those six nouns which when مُضَاف to any other noun besides the first person pronoun ى, will accept the اِعْرَاب بِالْحُرُوْف in the normal form of الْمُكَبَّرَة. However, in الْمُصَغَّرَة (diminutive form) they are given اِعْرَاب بِالْحَرَكَات. They are in total six nouns which are اَبٌ (father), اَخٌ (brother), حَمٌ (brother in-law), فَمٌ (mouth), هَنٌ (male private part) and ذُو (possessor, owner).

حالة الرفع	حالة النصب	حالة الجر
جَاءَ أَبُو زَيْدٍ	رَأَيْتُ أَبَا زَيْدٍ	مَرَرْتُ بِأَبِي زَيْدٍ
جَاءَنِي أَخُوكَ	رَأَيْتُ أَخَاكَ	مَرَرْتُ بِأَخِيكَ
جَاءَنِي حَمُوكِ	رَأَيْتُ حَمَاكِ	مَرَرْتُ بِحَمِيكِ
جَاءَنِي ذُوْمَالٍ	رَأَيْتُ ذَامَالٍ	مَرَرْتُ بِذِيْ مَالٍ
فُوكَ	فَاكَ	فِيكَ
فَمُكَ	فَمَكَ	فَمِكَ
هَنُوكَ	هَنَاكَ	هَنِيكَ

7) الْمُثَنَّى - Those nouns that are used to show dual form, e.g. رَجُلَانِ

8) كِلَا وَكِلْتَا - which mean 'both', however كِلَا is for masculine and كِلْتَا is used for feminine.

Note: Both words are usually Mudhāf to a Dhameer.

9) اِثْنَان وَ اِثْنَتَان - which mean 'two', however اِثْنَان is for masculine and اِثْنَتَان is for feminine.

<u>The إعْرَاب of the aforementioned words</u>
In the state of Raf'a it will be an Alif and in the state of Nasb and Jarr it will have a 'Yā' with a Fatha before it.

43

حالة الرفع	حالة النصب	حالة الجر
كِتَابَانِ	كِتَابَيْنِ	كِتَابَيْنِ
كِلَاهُمَا	كَلَيْهِمَا	كَلَيْهِمَا
كِلْتَاهُمَا	كِلْتَيْهِمَا	كِلْتَيْهِمَا
اِثْنَانِ	اِثْنَيْنِ	اِثْنَيْنِ
اِثْنَتَانِ	اِثْنَتَيْنِ	اِثْنَتَيْنِ

10) اَلْجَمْعُ الْمُذَكَّرُ السَّالِم - That masculine plural wherein the sequence of its singular form remains 'sound' and 'unbroken., e.g. مُسْلِمُوْنَ

11) أُولُو - This will always remain a Mudhāf, e.g. أُولُومَالٍ

12) The numbers from عِشْرُوْنَ to تِسْعُوْنَ (20 to 90).

The إِعْرَاب in the above three cases

In the state of Raf'a it will be a 'Waw' preceded by a Dhamma and in the state of Nasb and Jarr there will be a 'Yā' preceded by a Kasra.

حالة الرفع	حالة النصب	حالة الجر
مُسْلِمُوْنَ	مُسْلِمِيْنَ	مُسْلِمِيْنَ
عِشْرُوْنَ	عِشْرِيْنَ	عِشْرِيْنَ
أُولُومَالٍ	أُولِيْمَالٍ	أُولِيْمَالٍ

13) اَلْاِسْمُ الْمَقْصُوْرُ - That noun which has a small Alif at the end of the word e.g. عَصَا, مُوْسٰى.

The اِعْرَاب of اَلْاِسْمُ الْمَقْصُوْرُ will be hidden in all three cases.

14) اَلْجَمْعُ الْمُذَكَّرُ السَّالِمِ الْمُضَافِ اِلٰى يَاءِ الْمُتَكَلِّمِ - That masculine plural which is Mudhāf to the personal pronoun. The word مُسْلِمِيَّ was **originally** مُسْلِمُوْنِيْ. In reaching the final new form, the following steps were followed;

a) Because of the اِضَافَت the ن was discarded, thus it became مُسْلِمُوْىَ.

b) We now have a situation where a و and a ى are together. According to the rules of مَرْمِيٌّ the و is converted into a ى which is subsequently incorporated (اِدْغَام) into the already existent ى, therefore becoming مُسْلِمِيَّ.

c) The Dhamma on the 'Meem' is difficult to pronounce, hence it is converted into a Kasra because of the corresponding Harkat of the letter ى (at the end). Hence it becomes مُسْلِمِيَّ.

d) In the state of Nasb and Jarr the word will also be مُسْلِمِيَّ excluding the full need for the above process. However, in both these cases the اِعْرَاب is لَفْظِي i.e. apparent. This is because the word was originally مُسْلِمِيْنَ ى, because of اِضَافَت the ن was discarded becoming مُسْلِمِيْىَ. Thereafter the first ى was incorporated into the second ى, hence becoming مُسْلِمِيَّ.

The ruling will be that in the state of Raf'a there will be a hidden Dhamma rather than an apparent Dhamma whereas in the state of Nasb and Jarr, the إِعْرَاب will be apparent.

حَالَةُ الرَّفْع	هٰؤُلَاءِ مُسْلِمِیَّ
حَالَةُ النَّصْب	رَأَیْتُ مُسْلِمِیَّ
حَالَةُ الْجَرّ	مَرَرْتُ بِمُسْلِمِیَّ

15) ٱلْاِسْمُ الْمُضَافُ اِلٰی یَاءِ الْمُتَكَلِّم - That noun which is a Mudhāf to the first person pronoun ی. In all the cases, the إِعْرَاب will be hidden.

حَالَةُ الرَّفْع	جَآءَ وَلَدِیْ
حَالَةُ النَّصْب	رَأَیْتُ وَلَدِیْ
حَالَةُ الْجَرّ	مَرَرْتُ بِوَلَدِیْ

16) ٱلْاِسْمُ الْمَنْقُوْص - That noun which has a ی at the end preceded by a Kasra e.g. ٱلْقَاضِیْ.

حَالَةُ الرَّفْع	جَآءَ الْقَاضِیْ
حَالَةُ النَّصْب	رَأَیْتُ الْقَاضِیَ
حَالَةُ الْجَرّ	مَرَرْتُ بِالْقَاضِیْ

Note: In the state of Nasb, the Fatha will be لَفْظِی (apparent) and not تَقْدِیْرِی (hidden).

46

Exercise

Mention five examples of each اَلْأَسْمَاءُ الْمُعْرَبَة putting all its correct
إِعْرَاب.

Lesson 13: اَلْمَرْفُوعَات

Those words which are always Marfoo. They are in total 8 which
are as follows;

1) اَلْفَاعِلُ   2) نَائِبُ الْفَاعِلِ   3) اَلْمُبْتَدَا   4) اَلْخَبَرُ   5) اِسْمُ كَانَ وَأَخَوَاتِهَا
6) خَبَرُ لاَ الَّتِى لِنَفْىِ الْجِنْسِ   7) اِسْمُ مَا وَلاَ الْمُشَبَّهَتَيْنِ بِلَيْسَ   8) خَبَرُ إِنَّ وَأَخَوَاتِهَا

1) اَلْفَاعِل

اَلْفَاعِل is either the doer of the action e.g. نَصَرَ زَيْدٌ or it is the subject
with which the meaning conveyed by the فِعْل (verb) is found e.g.
عَلِمَ زَيْدٌ (Zaid knows). The فَاعِل is generally preceded by a فِعْل or a
word which resembles a فِعْل in effect and meaning which is known
as شِبْهُ الْفِعْل. Look at the following example.

زَيْدٌ عَالِمٌ أَبُوهُ

اَلْمُبْتَدَا

شِبْهُ الْفِعْلِ اَلْفَاعِلُ (مَرْفُوعٌ)

اَلْخَبَرُ

Below are some additional rules that apply to فِعْل and اَلْفَاعِلُ.

a) If اَلْفَاعِلُ is either a ظَاهِر مُؤَنَّث حَقِيقِي or ضَمِير مُؤَنَّث then the فعل will be a مُؤَنَّث (feminine). An example of ضَمِير مُؤَنَّث is; فَاطِمَةُ نَصَرَتْ ,هِنْدٌ قَامَتْ. An example of ظَاهِر مُؤَنَّث حَقِيقِي is; نَصَرَتْ فَاطِمَةُ ,قَامَتْ هِنْدٌ.

b) If اَلْفَاعِل is ظَاهِر جَمْع التَّكْسِير or ظَاهِر مُؤَنَّث غَيْر حَقِيقِي then the فِعْل can be either a مُؤَنَّث or مُذَكَّر. An example of ظَاهِر مُؤَنَّث غَيْر حَقِيقِي is; طَلَعَ الشَّمْسُ or it could be written as طَلَعَتِ الشَّمْسُ. An example of ظَاهِر جَمْع التَّكْسِير is; قَامَ الرِّجَالُ or قَامَتِ الرِّجَالُ.

c) If اَلْفَاعِل is ضَمِير جَمْع اَلْمُكَسَّر (hidden) then the فعل can be either a singular feminine or a plural masculine. For example; اَلرِّجَالُ قَامَتْ or اَلرِّجَالُ قَامُوا.

d) If اَلْفَاعِل is a ضَمِير then the فِعْل will be subject to the noun preceding it. For example; زَيْدٌ جَاءَ, زَيْدَانِ جَاءَا, زَيْدُونَ جَاءُوا.

e) If اَلْفَاعِل is ظَاهِر then the فِعْل will always be singular. For example; جَاءَ زَيْدٌ, جَاءَ زَيْدَانِ, جَاءَ زَيْدُونَ.

2) نَائِبُ الْفَاعِل

نَائِبُ الْفَاعِل is a noun which appears with a فِعْل مَجْهُول (a passive verb). It is usually called a نَائِبُ الْفَاعِل because it substitutes the فَاعِل. The

فَاعِل is not mentioned with a فِعْل مَجْهُوْل. For example; نُصِرَ زَيْدٌ.

Note: Those rules that apply to فِعْل and ٱلْفَاعِل are also applicable to نَائِبُ الْفَاعِل and فِعْل مَجْهُوْل. For example; نُصِرَتْ فَاطِمَةُ, فَاطِمَةُ نُصِرَتْ or نُصِرَ زَيْدٌ, نُصِرَ زَيْدَانِ, نُصِرَ زَيْدُوْنَ.

ٱلْمُبْتَدَا (3

ٱلْمُبْتَدَا is a noun that generally appears at the beginning of a sentence (ٱلْجُمْلَةُ الْإِسْمِيَّة) and has no visible عَامِل (governing agent) and its عَامِل is hidden. This hidden عَامِل is known as ٱلْإِبْتِدَاء (to begin). Therefore, the fact that the sentence starts with this اسْم would be a sufficient reason for it to be Marfoo.

ٱلْخَبَرُ (4

ٱلْخَبَرُ is a noun or a sentence which together with ٱلْمُبْتَدَا makes a complete meaningful sentence, e.g. زَيْدٌ عَالِمٌ.

اِسْمُ كَانَ وَأَخَوَاتِهَا (5

كَانَ and its similar أَفْعَال will appear before ٱلْجُمْلَةُ الْإِسْمِيَّة. It will give its اِسْم a Raf'a and its ٱلْخَبَر a Nasb. For example,

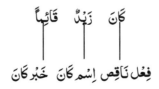

اَلْاَفْعَالُ اَلنَّاقِصَةُ are;

كَانَ، صَارَ، لَيْسَ، اَصْبَحَ، اَمْسَى، اَضْحَى، ظَلَّ، بَاتَ، مَادَامَ، مَازَالَ، مَابَرِحَ، مَاانْفَكَّ، مَافَتِئَ

(6) اِسْمُ مَاوَلَا الْمُشَبَّهَتَيْنِ بِلَيْسَ

The two letters مَا and لَا are similar in meaning and effect to لَيْسَ. They give its اِسْم a Raf'a and اَلْخَبَر a Nasb. مَا can come on both اَلْمَعْرِفَة and اَلنَّكِرَة for example, مَا زَيْدٌ قَائِماً and مَا رَجُلٌ قَائِماً whereas لَا will always come on اَلنَّكِرَة, for example; لَارَجُلٌ اَفْضَلَ مِنْكَ.

(7) خَبَرُ اِنَّ وَاَخَوَاتِهَا

اِنَّ and its similar particles appear before اَلْجُمْلَةُ الْاِسْمِيَّة. There are six in total, اِنَّ.اَنَّ (verily), لٰكِنَّ (but), كَاَنَّ (as though), لَعَلَّ (hopefully), لَيْتَ (wish). They give its اِسْم a Nasb and اَلْخَبَر a Raf'a. Some examples are as follows;

a) اِنَّ زَيْداً قَائِمٌ   اِنَّ اللهَ عَلِيْمٌ حَكِيْمٌ

b) عَلِمْتُ اَنَّ طَالِباً مَرِيْضٌ   وَاعْلَمُوْا اَنَّ اللهَ شَدِيْدُ الْعِقَابِ

c) زَيْدٌ حَاضِرٌ وَلٰكِنَّ عَمْرٌو غَائِبٌ   وَلٰكِنَّ الشَّيَاطِيْنَ كَفَرُوْا

d) كَاَنَّ زَيْداً نَائِمٌ

e) لَعَلَّ الْمُدَرِّسَ حَاضِرٌ   لَعَلَّ اللهَ يُحْدِثُ بَعْدَ ذٰلِكَ اَمْراً

f) لَيْتَ زَيْداً قَائِمٌ

(8) خَبَرُ لَاَالَّتِي لِنَفْي الْجِنْس

The خَبَر of that لا which excludes a complete جِنْس (genus). It gives its اِسْم a Nasb and خَبَر a Raf'a only when the following two conditions are met;

a) Both the اِسْم and the خَبَر are اَلنَّكِرَة.

b) The اِسْم precedes the خَبَر, e.g. لَارَجُلَ فِى الدَّارِ.

Exercise

Give five examples of each type of Marfoo by putting their correct اِعْرَاب.

Lesson 14: اَلْمَنْصُوبَات

Those words which are always Mansoob. They are:

(1) اَلْمَفْعُوْلُ بِهِ   (2) اَلْمَفْعُوْلُ الْمُطْلَق   (3) اَلْمَفْعُوْلُ لَهُ   (4) اَلْمَفْعُوْلُ فِيْهِ
(5) اَلْمَفْعُوْلُ مَعَهُ   (6) اَلْحَالُ   (7) اَلتَّمْيِيْزُ   (8) خَبَرُ كَانَ وَأَخَوَاتِهَا
(9) خَبَرُ مَا وَلَا الْمُشَبَّهَتَيْنِ بِلَيْسَ   (10) اِسْمُ اِنَّ وَأَخَوَاتِهَا   (11) اَلْمُسْتَثْنَى
(12) اِسْمُ لَا الَّتِي لِنَفْي الْجِنْس

(1) اَلْمَفْعُوْلُ بِهِ

اَلْمَفْعُوْلُ بِهِ is that word upon which the action takes place. Its عَامل is اَلْفِعْلُ الْمُتَعَدِّى or any word with a similar effect to it. Some examples are as follows;

a) ضَرَبَ زَيْدٌ عَمْروًا (اَلْفِعْلُ ٱلْمُتَعَدِّى)

b) عَلَيْكُمْ اَنْفُسَكُمْ (اِسْمُ الْفِعْلِ)

c) وَلَوْ لَا دَفْعُ اللهِ النَّاسَ (اَلْمَصْدَرِ)

2) اَلْمَفْعُوْلُ الْمُطْلَقُ

اَلْمَفْعُوْلُ الْمُطْلَقُ is actually the مَصْدَر of the فِعْل mentioned before it. For example; ضَرَبْتُ ضَرْبًا. It serves any of the following purposes;

a) تَأْكِيْد (Emphasis) e.g. وَكَلَّمَ اللهُ مُوْسَى تَكْلِيْمًا, ضَرَبْتُهُ ضَرْبًا (Indeed Allāh ﷻ spoke to Mūsā ﷺ).

b) بَيَانُ النَّوْع (Manner of action) e.g. جَلَسْتُ جِلْسَةَ الْقَارِى (I sat in the manner of a Qāri).

c) بَيَانُ الْعَدَد (Number of times) e.g. ضَرَبْتُ ضَرْبَتَيْنِ (I hit him with two blows)

3) اَلْمَفْعُوْلُ لَهُ

اَلْمَفْعُوْلُ لَهُ is that اِسْم which explains the reason for the فِعْل to occur. For example, ضَرَبْتُهُ تَأْدِيْبًا (I hit him to teach him manners), قُمْتُ لَهُ اِكْرَامًا (I stood for him out of respect).

4) اَلْمَفْعُوْلُ مَعَهُ

اَلْمَفْعُوْلُ مَعَهُ is that اِسْم which appears after such a وَاو that shows companionship and connection. This وَاو is referred to as وَاوُ الْمُصَاحَبَة. For example, جَآءَ زَيْدٌ وَالْكِتَابَ (Zaid came with the book), جَآءَ الْبَرْدُ وَالْجُبَّاتِ (The cold appeared with the clothing).

5) ٱلْمَفْعُوْلُ فِيْهِ

ٱلْمَفْعُوْلُ فِيْهِ is such an اِسْم that shows its time and place in which the action takes place. For example; صُمْتُ شَهْرًا (I fasted for a month), دَخَلْتُ الْمَسْجِدَ (I entered the Masjid).

6) ٱلْحَالُ

ٱلْحَالُ is a circumstantial expression or phrase. Such expressions could be:

a) In a single word e.g. جَاءَ زَيْدٌ رَاكِبًا (Zaid came riding)

b) In a sentence e.g. جَاءَ زَيْدٌ وَهُوَ رَاكِبٌ (Zaid came whilst he was riding).

There are some additional rules relating to the حَال;

a)   حَال can describe the state of the فَاعِل, e.g. جَاءَ زَيْدٌ رَاكِبًا.

b)   Or the state of the مَفْعُوْل, e.g. جِئْتُ زَيْدًا نَائِمًا (I came whilst Zaid was sleeping)

c)   Or sometimes describes the state of both the فَاعِل and مَفْعُوْل, e.g. لَقِيْتُ زَيْدًا رَاكِبَيْنِ (I met Zaid whilst we were both riding)

7) ٱلتَّمْيِيْزُ

ٱلتَّمْيِيْزُ is an اِسْمُ النَّكِرَة which removes the ambiguity that emerges by the preceding اِسْم. The مُبْهَم (ambiguous) اِسْم preceding it may show any of the following;

a) A number e.g. عِنْدِىْ اَحَدَ عَشَرَ كِتَابًا (I have eleven books)

53

b) A distance e.g. عِنْدِى شِبْرٌ أَرْضًا (I have one span of land)

c) A measurement e.g. عِنْدِى رِطْلٌ زَيْتًا (I have one litre of oil)

d) Something that has been derived from the تَمْيِيز e.g. هٰذَا خَاتَمٌ حَدِيْدًا (This is a ring of iron)

e) An unclear phrase e.g. أَنَا أَكْثَرُ مِنْكَ مَالًا (I have more wealth than you)

خَبْرُ كَانَ وَأَخَوَاتِهَا (8

This has been previously discussed in Lesson 13 under the section of إِسْمُ كَانَ وَأَخَوَاتِهَا. For example كَانَ زَيْدٌ قَائِمًا. The ٱلْخَبْر will have a Fatha.

ٱلْخَبْرُ مَا وَلَا ٱلْمُشَبَّهَتَيْنِ بِلَيْسَ (9

This has also been discussed previously under the section of إِسْمُ مَا وَلَا ٱلْمُشَبَّهَتَيْنِ بِلَيْسَ in Lesson 13. For example مَا رَجُلٌ قَائِمًا. The ٱلْخَبْر will have a Fatha on it.

إِسْمُ إِنَّ وَأَخَوَاتِهَا (10

This has also been discussed in Lesson 13 under the section of خَبْرُ إِنَّ وَأَخَوَاتِهَا. For example إِنَّ اللهَ عَلِيْمٌ حَكِيْمٌ. The إِسْم will have a Fatha on it.

إِسْمُ لَا ٱلَّتِى لِنَفْىِ الْجِنْس (11

This has been discussed previously under the section of خَبْرُ لَا ٱلَّتِى لِنَفْىِ الْجِنْس. For example لَا رَجُلَ فِى الدَّارِ. It will give the إِسْم a Fatha.

12) ٱلْمُسْتَثْنَى

This means to exclude something. The noun that shows the exempted thing is called ٱلْمُسْتَثْنَى and the word from which something has been exempted from is called ٱلْمُسْتَثْنَى مِنْهُ. For example;

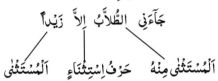

جَاءَنِي الطُّلاَّبُ اِلاَّ زَيْداً

ٱلْمُسْتَثْنَى مِنْهُ   حَرْفُ اِسْتِثْنَاءٍ   ٱلْمُسْتَثْنَى

Exercise

Give three examples of each ٱلْمَنْصُوبَات and explain their اِعْرَاب also.

Lesson 15: اَلْمَجْرُوْرَات

There are only two اَلْمَجْرُوْرَات which are as follows;

1) اَلْمَجْرُوْرُ بِالْحُرُوْفِ الْجَارَّةِ

2) اَلْمَجْرُوْرُ بِالْإِضَافَةِ

1) اَلْحُرُوْفُ الْجَارَّةُ (Preposition letters)

These are those letters that give the word coming after it a Kasra. The noun that comes after the اَلْجَرِّ letter will be called اَلْمَجْرُوْر. For example;

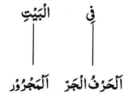

فِي الْبَيْتِ

اَلْحَرْفُ الْجَرِّ اَلْمَجْرُوْر

There are in total 17 letters that will give the following word a Kasra;

ب، ت، ك، ل، وَ، مُذ، مُنْذُ، خَلاَ، رُبَّ، حَاشَا، مِنْ، عَدَا، فِي، عَن، عَلَى، حَتّى، إِلَى

Some examples are as follows;

a) ب - e.g. خَرَجْتُ بِزَيْدٍ (I went with Zaid)

b) ت - e.g. تَاللهِ (By Allāh)

c) ك - e.g. زَيْدٌ كَالْأَسَدِ (Zaid is like a lion)

d) ل - e.g. قُمْتُ لِزَيْدٍ (I stood up for Zaid)

e) وَ - e.g. وَاللهِ (By Allāh)

f) مُذْ وَ مُنْذُ —both have similar meaning e.g. مُنْذُ شَهْرٍ (Since a month)

g) خَلاَ - e.g. جَاءَ الطُّلاَّبُ خَلاَ زَيْدٍ (The students came except Zaid)

h) رُبَّ - e.g. رُبَّ قَارِئٍ الْقُرْآنِ وَالْقُرْآنُ يَلْعَنُهُ (Many are reciters of the Holy Qur'ān but the Qur'ān curses them)

i) حَاشَا - e.g. جَاءَ الطُّلاَّبُ حَاشَا زَيْدٍ (The students came except Zaid)

j) مِنْ - e.g. سِرْتُ مِنَ الْبَصْرَةِ (I travelled from Basra)

k) عَدَا - same as حَاشَا and خَلاَ.

l) فِي - e.g. زَيْدٌ فِي الدَّارِ (Zaid is in the house)

m) عَنْ - e.g. سَأَلْتُهُ عَنِ الدَّرْسِ (I asked him about the lesson)

n) عَلَى - e.g. ٱلْكِتَابُ عَلَى الْمَكْتَبِ (The book is on the table)

o) حَتَّى - e.g. أَكَلْتُ السَّمَكَةَ حَتَّى رَأْسِهَا (I ate the fish including its head)

p) اِلَى - e.g. ذَهَبْتُ اِلَى الْمَسْجِدِ (I went to the Masjid)

2) ٱلْمَجْرُوْرُ بِالْإِضَافَةِ

This is a phrase wherein the words are generally related to one another by showing possession. The first word is called ٱلْمُضَاف and the second ٱلْمُضَاف إِلَيْهِ. For example; كِتَابُ زَيْدٍ (Zaid's book), in this example ٱلْمُضَاف is كِتَابُ and ٱلْمُضَاف إِلَيْهِ is زَيْدٍ.

Some additional rules relating to ٱلْمَجْرُوْرُ بِالْإِضَافَةِ:

a) The إِعْرَاب of ٱلْمُضَاف depends upon the governing word that precedes it, however ٱلْمُضَاف إِلَيْهِ will always remain a Majroor e.g.

بِسْمِ اللّٰهِ. In this example اَلْمُضَاف has been given a Kasra because of the letter ب preceding it.

b) اَلْمُضَاف is never prefixed with a ال and neither will it have a Tanween on it. However, اَلْمُضَاف اِلَيْه can accept both e.g. كِتَابُ طَالِبٍ, كِتَابُ الطَّالِبِ.

Exercise

1) Mention three examples of اَلْحُرُوف الْجَارَّة preferably from the Qur'ān and Hadeeth.

2) Give five examples of اَلْمَجْرُوْر بِالإِضَافَة preferably from the Qur'ān and Hadeeth.

Lesson 16: اَلتَّوَابِعُ

A noun is usually governed by the عَامِل that precedes it and sometimes a word that comes after the noun follows the same governing إِعْرَاب that applies to the noun. When this is the case then the إِعْرَاب which is applied to the preceding noun (which is called اَلْمَتْبُوْع) will also be found on اَلتَّابِع (the follower). For example;

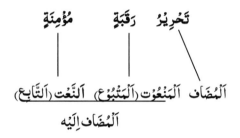

In the above example the word مُؤْمِنَةٍ is following up the same governing إِعْرَاب as that of رَقَبَةٍ. Both words have the same عَامِل.

There are five categories of اَلتَّوَابِع;

1) اَلنَّعْت (صِفَة) - Adjective

2) اَلتَّأْكِيْد - Emphasis

3) اَلبَدَل - Substitute

4) عَطْفُ البَيَان

5) اَلْعَطْفُ بِحَرْفٍ

1) اَلنَّعْتُ (اَلصِّفَةُ)

اَلنَّعْت is that تَابِع which describes the state of اَلْمَنْعُوت, e.g. رَجُلٌ فَاضِلٌ, اَلرَّجُلُ الصَّالِحُ, اَلْمَرْأَةُ الصَّالِحَةُ.

اَلنَّعْت must correspond to اَلْمَنْعُوت in four major aspects;

a) إِعْرَاب   b) Gender   c) Quantity (singular, dual and plural)
d) Mārifah and Nakirah

Some examples are; رَجُلٌ صَالِحٌ, رَجُلَانِ صَالِحَانِ, رِجَالٌ صَالِحُونَ,
بِنْتٌ صَالِحَةٌ, بِنْتَانِ صَالِحَتَانِ, بَنَاتٌ صَالِحَاتٌ, اَلرَّجُلُ الصَّالِحُ, اَلْمَرْأَةُ الصَّالِحَةُ.

2) اَلتَّأْكِيدُ

اَلتَّأْكِيد is that تَابِع which emphasises the meaning conveyed by the فِعل and which is confined by the اَلْمَتْبُوع only. For example; جَاءَ زَيْدٌ نَفْسُهُ, in this example the word نَفْسُهُ is emphasising the meaning conveyed by the فعل about زَيْدٌ. It can also come to confirm the inclusion of all the members of the اَلْمَتْبُوع, for example; فَسَجَدَ الْمَلَائِكَةُ كُلُّهُمْ.

There are two types of اَلتَّأْكِيد;

1: اَلتَّأْكِيدُ اللَّفْظِي - This type of emphasis occurs by the repetition of words. The repetition of words can be either;

a) فِعل - e.g. جَاءَ جَاءَ زَيْدٌ
b) إِسْم - e.g. جَاءَ زَيْدٌ زَيْدٌ

60

c) حَرْف - e.g. اِنَّ زَيْدًا قَائِمٌ

d) ضَمِيْر - e.g. ذَهَبَ هُوَ

2: اَلتَّاكِيْدُ الْمَعْنَوِى - This type of emphasis is achieved by the following words;

a) نَفْس - e.g. جَاءَنِى زَيْدٌ نَفْسُهُ

b) عَيْن - e.g. جَاءَنِى زَيْدٌ عَيْنُهُ

3) اَلبَدْلُ (Substitute)

اَلبَدْلُ is that تَابِع which is the actual focus of reference in the sentence. The اَلْمَتْبُوْع merely serves as an introduction to the تَابِع. The تَابِع is called اَلبَدْل and the اَلْمَتْبُوْع is called اَلْمُبَدَل مِنْهُ.

This can be understood in the following example;

There are four types of اَلبَدْل;

a) بَدْلُ الْكُل b) بَدْلُ البَعْض c) بَدْلُ الْإِشْتِمَال d) بَدْلُ الْغَلَط

a) بَدْلُ الْكُل - It is that اَلبَدْل which is identical in the purpose to that of اَلْمُبَدَل مِنْهُ as in the above mentioned example. In the Holy Qur'ān

Allāh ﷻ states,

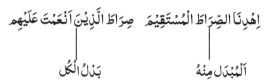

(Guide us to the straight path; the path of those whom You have favoured)

b) بَدَلُ البَعْض - It is that اَلبَدَل which is part of the اَلْمُبْدَل مِنْهُ. For example ضَرَبْتُ زَيْدًا رَأْسَهُ. It is stated in the Holy Qur'ān,

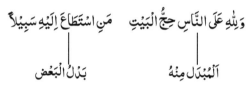

(And Hajj to the House of Allāh is a duty upon mankind owing to Allāh those who can afford the expenses towards it).

c) بَدَلُ الْإِشْتِمَال - It is that type of اَلبَدَل which is in some way associated with the اَلْمُبْدَل مِنْهُ. For example سُرِقَ زَيْدٌ ثَوْبُهُ (Zaid, his clothes has been stolen). In the Holy Qur'ān it is stated;

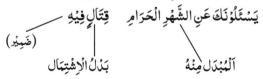

(They ask you regarding the sacred month, i.e. waging war in them)

Note: In the case of بَدَلُ البَعَض and بَدَلُ الإِشْتِمَال there must be a ضَمِير (pronoun) in the بَدَل which refers back to the اَلْمُبَدَل مِنْهُ.

d) بَدَلُ الْغَلَط - It is that اَلبَدَل which corrects the mistake of an error caused by the slip of the tongue in اَلْمُبَدَل مِنْهُ. In other words, اَلْمُبَدَل مِنْهُ was not intended. For example رَأَيْتُ زَيْداً خَالِداً (I saw Zaid, rather Khalid).

Note: When correcting the mistake it is preferable to prefix the word بَل before the اَلبَدَل i.e. to say بَل خَالِداً.

4) عَطْفُ البَيَان

عَطْفُ البَيَان is that تَابِع which merely clarifies and specifies its اَلْمَتْبُوع. For example; كَتَبَ أَبُو حَفْصٍ عُمَرُ. In this example the word عُمَرُ is عَطْفُ البَيَان. It is stated in the Holy Qur'ān.

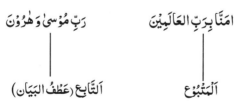

رَبِّ مُوْسٰى وَ هٰرُوْنَ   اٰمَنَّا بِرَبِّ العَالَمِيْنَ

اَلتَّابِع (عَطْفُ البَيَان)   اَلْمَتْبُوع

(We have believed in the Lord of the worlds, the Lord of Moosā and Hārūn)

‫5)‬ اَلْعَطْفُ بِحَرْفٍ

It is that اَلتَّابِع whereby a conjunction letter (حَرْف عَطْف) is used between the اَلتَّابِع and the اَلْمَتْبُوع to form a connection between them both. For example;

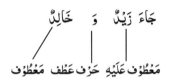

جَاءَ زَيْدٌ   وَ   خَالِدٌ

مَعْطُوْف عَلَيْهِ   حَرْف عَطْف   مَعْطُوْف

Here the verb (جَاءَ) is directed to both the مَعْطُوْف and the مَعْطُوْف عَلَيْهِ.

Exercise

Give five examples of each of the different types of اَلتَّوَابِع preferably from the Holy Qur'ān and Ahādeeth with their إِعْرَاب.

64